101
WAYS TO
LIVE WELL

Mindfulness, yoga and nutrition tips for busy people

Contents

Busy? Stressed? Downright frazzled?
The wellness tips in this book provide tangible
solutions to the stresses and strains of everyday
life. That means ditching the generic, one-size-
fits-all approach and embracing the targeted,
let's-get-this-sorted attitude, with tips from
experts covering everything from craving-crushing
snacks and yoga twists to stimulate digestion and
mindfulness exercises to help you sleep better.

Of course, we don't all have the luxury of enough
free time to become a yogi master or meditation
expert. This book promises to help you declutter
your brain in the most efficient way possible. So
whether it's on your daily commute, in your lunch-
hour break or in the checkout queue, use these
techniques to become a calmer, more productive
and happier you – whatever life throws your way.

TIPS FOR THE BODY

 Health & exercise

 Nutrition

TIPS FOR THE MIND

 Mindfulness

Communication

Invigorate your body

The Sun Salutation is a morning yoga practice to get the blood flowing and stretch all the major muscles, awakening the whole body. Yoga teacher Amanda Fell (amandafellyoga.com) explains how.

1. Stand tall with feet together and palms touching each other in front of the chest.

2. Inhale, raise the arms and gently bend backwards, stretching the arms above the head.

3. Exhale and slowly bend forwards so your head meets your knees and your hands reach your feet (or as far as they can go).

4. Inhaling deeply, take a long backwards step with the right leg. Keep your hands and feet firmly on the ground, with the left foot positioned between the hands. Look up to the sky.

5. While exhaling, take the left foot to meet the right one. Keeping your arms straight, raise the hips and position the head in between the arms.

6. Hold your breath and lower the entire body to the floor until your feet, knees, hands, chest and forehead touch the ground.

7. Inhale, and lift the torso to bend it backwards, and look towards the sky.

8. Exhale and push the hips towards the ceiling, keeping the arms straight.

9. Inhale and step the right leg between your hands.

10. Exhale and bring your left leg to join the right. Repeat step 3.

11. Inhale and repeat step 2.

12. Exhale and return to the starting position. Repeat the sequence eight times, alternating between legs.

Kick-start your day

Smoothies are
a quick, easy way to
create a breakfast-to-go
that contains the perfect
balance of protein, healthy
fats and micronutrients,
alongside the fruit fibre
that juicing removes.

Steal nutritionist Rhiannon Lambert's (rhitrition.com) smoothie recipe. Fill your blender or smoothie-maker with ½ avocado, ⁴/₅ cup (200mL) unsweetened almond milk, a handful of spinach, a handful of frozen berries, a small cube of fresh ginger (depending on how much you like its zing) and 1 tsp (5mL) barley grass powder. Whizz to a smooth consistency, adding a little water if you prefer a thinner texture. Pour into a tall glass and top with a few goji berries.

Elevate your motivation

Music has been shown to elicit specific psychological responses, depending upon the type of song played. This means that the right playlist can retune your mindset entirely.

Improve your motivation or positive attitude by listening to music that evinces a positive emotional response in you. Try to schedule a time every day during which you play a selection of songs, channelling your focus on the music rather than any external stimuli. Notice if there are certain tunes that make you feel happy or more positive or focused. Take note of these, add them to a playlist on your computer or phone, then play them regularly to improve your mood and confidence.

Boost your energy

Maca root is
a South American
plant naturally high in
amino acids, minerals and
phytonutrients that has
traditionally been used for its
hormone-balancing and
stamina-enhancing
properties.

Thanks to its sweet, caramel-like taste,
maca powder can easily be incorporated into
breakfast to energise your body for the day ahead.
Throw 1 small frozen banana, 1 handful of baby
spinach, 2 tsp (10mL) nut butter, 2 tsp (10mL)
maca and a big glug of almond milk into a blender
and blitz until smooth for a pick-me-up
breakfast milkshake.

Lift your mood

The scent of jasmine oil has been proven to have an arousing effect on the body, increasing breathing rate, blood pressure and oxygen levels in the blood.

To feel more alert and uplifted, mix jasmine essential oil with a carrier oil (almond works well) and use your fingertips to rub a little of the mixture on to your temples, down your nose and on to your décolletage or chest area. The natural heat of the body will help disperse the scent into the air. Alternatively, if you're not into massage oils, choose an indoor candle scented with jasmine and light it for 20 minutes to allow the smell to permeate throughout the room.

Stimulate your digestion

Yoga twists massage the organs within the abdominal cavity, which awakens and invigorates them to act more efficiently, says expert Amanda Fell.

04

First thing in the morning, on an empty stomach, lie on your back. Inhaling, draw the right knee up into the chest, pulling it in tight with your arms. Let the right arm rest on the floor alongside your body, palm downwards. Use your left hand to gently move your bent right knee over to the left side. Keep both shoulders firmly to the floor and twist through the centre of your waist, utilising the obliques. Breathe into the pose, twisting deeper with your next exhale. Repeat on the opposite side.

Stave off toothache

Cloves contain the active ingredient eugenol – a natural pain-reliever used in some over-the-counter pain rubs.

Applying clove oil – available from supermarkets and health shops – to a cotton bud and rubbing it on your gums can temporarily ease toothache pain until you can get to a dentist. However, don't go overboard or use it for a prolonged period of time, as too much can cause side effects to both your gums and your body as a whole. Alternatively, popping a little clove powder into your evening curry might be a more appetising way to numb the pain.

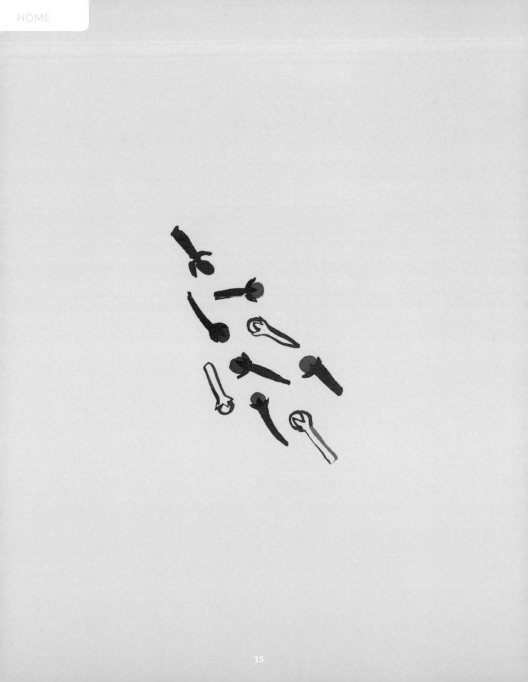

Relieve stiff joints

Avocados contain phytosterols, carotenoid antioxidants and omega-3 fatty acids, which make the fruit an anti-inflammatory agent.

Cut 1 avocado in half and scoop the flesh into a bowl. Add a squeeze of lime juice and season with a little salt and pepper. Using the back of a spoon, roughly smash the avocado until it is chunky but spreadable. Smooth over a slice of toast. For extra protein, top with a poached egg.

Spice up your life

Turmeric has powerful antioxidant and anti-inflammatory properties, which help to prevent disease, the effects of ageing and brain conditions.

The must-have seasoning of the moment, turmeric can be added to curries, vegetable soups or plain boiled rice to add both colour and taste. One of the easiest ways to work it on to your plate is to spice up your breakfast eggs, suggests nutritionist Rhiannon Lambert. Add 1 tsp (5mL) turmeric, and some chilli flakes if you can handle the heat, to your scrambled eggs to fire up your morning.

Bolster positivity

Even brief interactions with pets increase the body's level of oxytocin, a brain chemical that increases humans' ability to solve problems and create meaningful social interactions.

Got a pet? Ensure you make time to play with it every day for at least a few minutes. Don't have an animal to call your own? Look into the possibility of fostering a pet or 'borrowing' one from owners local to you, to ease their load and reap the benefits yourself. Apps like borrowmydoggy.com can help, or contact your local rescue centre to enquire if they need volunteers.

Win the germ war

Ensuring proper hand hygiene is the primary way to reduce the spread of infections and diseases.

Most of us don't wash our hands nearly as often or as thoroughly as we should. Wet your hands with clean running water (warm or cold), turn off the tap and apply soap. Lather your hands together with the soap, including the backs of the hands, between the fingers and under the nails, scrubbing well. This process should last about as long as it takes you to sing 'Happy Birthday' from beginning to end twice. Rinse your hands well, then dry them on a clean towel or leave them to air dry.

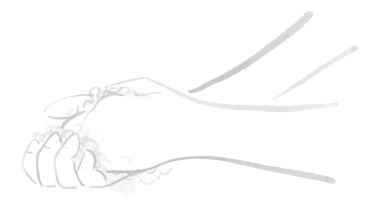

Hijack hay fever

Carotenoids, the natural plant pigments responsible for giving carrots, pumpkins and sweet potatoes their orange hue, reduce inflammation of the airways and bolster the immune system.

Eating one or two servings of carotenoid-rich food every day should stand you in good stead. For an easy dinner, scrub a sweet potato, prick it with a fork and cook it until tender in the microwave for 10–18 minutes (the time will depend upon its size – check it at regular intervals). Cut the sweet potato in half lengthways and place it flesh-side up on a plate. Top with steamed asparagus, spinach, crumbled feta cheese, finely chopped spring onions and black pepper.

Join the meat-free Monday club

Incorporating just one veggie-friendly day into your week if you're a big meat-eater can help decrease your risk of heart disease, cancer and stroke.

Try this tagine from Rhiannon Lambert. Chop 4 carrots, 4 parsnips, 4 red onions and 2 red peppers into chunks. Scatter on a baking tray, drizzle with olive oil and roast in the oven at 200°C/390°F for 30 minutes. Meanwhile, fry spices with olive oil in a pan, then add 400g (14oz) canned chopped tomatoes, a handful of chopped beetroot, 200g (7oz) drained canned chickpeas, a small sprinkle of raisins and $1^2/_3$ cups (400mL) water. Simmer for 5 minutes, stir in the veg and serve with quinoa.

Ease headache tension

This hair-pulling technique loosens the scalp's fascia – a layer of connective tissue that covers the skull and surrounding muscles – which releases tension and eases nerve pressure.

Take a large handful of hair at the crown of your head and pull it away from the scalp. Use a gentle motion to begin with, but pull enough that you feel a slight discomfort. Hold for a few seconds, or until you can feel any discomfort decrease. Release the hair and move on to another section, until all the hair has been pulled. For a deeper release, repeat the process, but instead of pulling the hair directly away from the head turn it in a clockwise direction while gently pulling away from the skull.

Freshen up your water intake

One of the most common excuses for not drinking the recommended eight glasses a day is that people find plain water boring. The solution? Transform it into a fruit-infused tonic.

For a refreshing drink, slice a handful of fresh strawberries, a 5cm (2in) chunk of cucumber and 2 limes. Take a large glass jug and layer the fruit, along with a small handful of fresh mint leaves, with ice cubes. Next, fill the jug with water and pop it in the fridge to infuse. Fancy something more fragrant? Fill a large jug with water and add 2 large handfuls of blueberries and a generous sprinkling of edible lavender flowers. Cover and chill until ready to drink, then strain, add ice and sup up.

Ease menstrual pain

Increasing calcium intake can reduce PMS symptoms by 30 per cent because the usual suspects – fatigue, cramping, headaches and irritability – are often linked to a deficiency of the mineral.

It's better to get your calcium boost from whole foods rather than supplements; aim to add two extra portions of calcium-rich food to your diet every day. As well as dairy sources such as yoghurt, cheese and milk, dark leafy greens, tofu, quinoa and soft-boned fish (such as sardines and canned salmon) are also high in calcium and have the added bonus of supplying magnesium, which allows the calcium to be optimally absorbed into the body.

Treat yourself

This warming drink from nutritionist Rhiannon Lambert is a low-cal version of hot chocolate, with the energising and anti-oxidising benefits of raw cacao.

Warm 2$^1/_3$ cups (550mL) of almond, coconut or hemp milk in a saucepan on a low heat. Add a vanilla pod and 2 tsp (10mL) raw cacao powder, and stir until the powder has fully dissolved. Continue to heat, without boiling the milk, for 5 minutes, then remove the vanilla pod and pour it into a mug. Dust with a sprinkle of cacao powder to serve – to make it that bit more indulgent – and drink up.

Embrace downtime

This mindfulness practice from expert James Milford (themindfulmethod.co.uk) settles the mind and encourages acceptance that relaxing and restful activities are essential for health.

Lie with your arms at your sides, feet falling away from each other. Become aware of the points at which the body is supported, and of the breath. Silently repeat the phrase: 'Nowhere to be, nothing to do, nothing to strive for, just resting as I am.' Now bring your awareness down to the feet and focus your attention with a sense of curiosity about any physical sensations. Then bring the focus to the ankles, the lower legs and so on to the head. Finally expand the awareness to the whole body.

Learn to sleep better

James Milford suggests that this simple breathing exercise settles a busy mind and helps you to accept, rather than fight, the reality of having trouble sleeping.

Lying down, bring the awareness to the belly and focus on the sensations of the breath. Feel how the muscles tighten and release and how the torso moves. After a few moments, place both hands on your belly. Become aware of the sensations under your hands as the belly rises and falls. To aid concentration, on each in-breath count '1', then '2', and continue until you reach 10. Once you reach 10, go back to 1 and keep counting breaths in a cycle until the end of the practice.

Stop night-time indigestion

Lying on your back ensures that the oesophagus sits above the stomach, making it less likely that food or other substances will move back up the body.

If you're used to sleeping on your side, try to fall asleep with your body in a straight line and your back on the mattress. This allows the head, neck and spine to align in a neutral position, adding no extra pressure to the spine or curves in the vertebrae. Not only will this reduce the risk of indigestion and heartburn, but it's also key to avoiding back pain, too. Be aware, however, that sleeping this way can worsen snoring, so it's not ideal for everyone.

Have a calmer commute

This
meditation exercise
from expert Mark Leonard
(mindfulness4change.com)
will reduce the stress of
commuting. You can do it
on the train platform,
at the bus stop or
before driving.

Stand with your feet parallel and about hip-width apart, your knees slightly bent and arms hanging loosely. Pay attention to the feelings on the soles of the feet. Notice sensations of breathing in and breathing out. With your awareness grounded in the body, turn your attention to the sounds in the space around you. Note thoughts, label sounds, then allow them to just come and go in the mind. Acknowledge the urge to be distracted, returning your focus again to your posture.

Healthify your morning high

Tweaking the time at which you drink your usual cup of coffee can help increase its positive effects on your energy levels and its disease-busting properties.

The body's naturally high levels of cortisol (the stress hormone) first thing in the morning mean that drinking a cuppa then not only lowers the levels of hormone production, which leaves you flagging, but increases your tolerance to caffeine. Save your coffee fix for late morning – between 10am and noon – and afternoon – between 2pm and 5pm – to maintain the body's natural hormone balance and get the most from your pick-me-up cup.

Speak confidently in public

This practice from James Milford (themindfulmethod. co.uk) encourages you to acknowledge and accept fear rather than treating it as something to be suppressed or defeated.

Whenever you feel nervous in the lead-up to a public-speaking event, stand or sit in a quiet place. Begin by bringing awareness to your breath. Next, bring to mind the public speaking you have to do and notice the physical reactions that occur in the body, allowing them to play out and fade of their own accord. Allow yourself to feel the fear without reacting to it. Try this a few times to familiarise yourself with the feelings of anxiety, before returning to your natural breath to settle the mind.

Up your calorie burn

Foregoing the
lift in favour of the stairs
is a simple, effective way to
increase your heart rate and
calorie-burn throughout the
working day.

Want to upgrade the positive effects of taking the more traditional way of travelling between floors? Resist striding up two stairs at a time; research shows that walking up every single step burns more calories because the energy turnover within the body is increased with a greater number of smaller steps.

Crush morning cravings

Eating regularly throughout the day is crucial to maintaining a healthy metabolism and avoiding fluctuations in blood sugar, says nutritionist Rhiannon Lambert (rhitrition.com).

Create a snack that combines fibre and protein with Rhiannon's handmade protein bar recipe: mash together ½ banana and 2 tbs (30mL) coconut oil. In another bowl, mix 1 cup (100g) oats, 2 tsp (10g) berries, 1 tbs (15g) seeds and 1 tbs (15g) chopped apricots. Combine the mixtures along with 1 tsp (5mL) stevia and 1 tbs (15mL) nut butter. Press the mixture on to a greased baking tray so that it is about 1.5cm ($^3/_5$in) thick and bake at 180°C (350°F) for 20 minutes.

Cute concentration-boosters

Research shows that looking at cute images not only enhances mood but also improves performance for tasks that require concentration.

The perfect excuse to seek out those puppy memes! Looking at baby animals triggers our biological predisposition to respond to infant features (the so-called 'baby schema'), such as a large head, protruding forehead and large eyes – and indirectly improves attention skills. Change your computer desktop image to show cute animals or flick through six or seven different images on the web when you're particularly prone to procrastination.

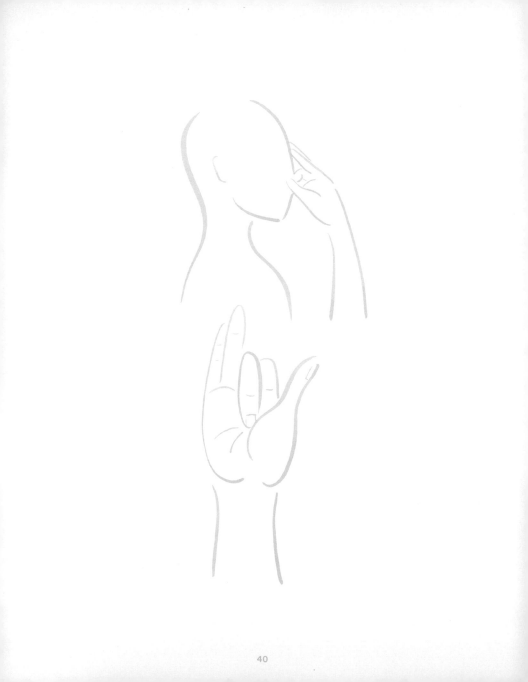

Stress less

This yoga breathing practice from teacher Amanda Fell (amandafellyoga.com) guides the mind to let go of anxieties that may cloud judgement and reduces natural responses to stress.

Sit comfortably with your spine upright and head in line. Relax the whole body and close your eyes. Place the thumb and ring finger of the right hand on your nostrils with the index and forefinger resting on the forehead. Begin by inhaling deeply to maximum capacity through the right nostril as you close the left one with your finger. Then block the right nostril before breathing out slowly through the left one. Repeat on the opposite side, for 5–10 rounds.

Stimulate the mind

Cinnamon has been proven to boost brainpower, specifically improving focus, memory and cognitive processing.

The spice's brain-related benefits stand both when it's eaten as a food or smelled as a scent. For a morning lift, sprinkle some ground cinnamon on top of warm porridge to target both senses. Don't like the taste? Pick up some cinnamon essential oil from high-street health shops and, after diluting it with a carrier oil, rub a small amount on to your temples and neck to smell subtly throughout the day.

Take a better break

Research indicates that hitting the pause button and taking your allocated break earlier in the working day increases energy levels and enhances productivity.

Try to schedule your break for mid-morning (or the equivalent if you work shifts) for just one day, and see what effect it has. Experts also suggest that to feel the most refreshed and satisfied after a break at work, an individual has to set the agenda for their free time *themselves*. So take that time earlier in the day to do what you want to do, whether that's staying at your desk to finish a project that you care about, calling a friend to catch up or fitting in an exercise session.

Eat clever for energy

Snacks that contain a good balance of fibre and natural fats stimulate the body without the speedy highs and sluggish lows caused by sugar and caffeine.

Beat the afternoon slump by spreading a teaspoon of your favourite nut butter (make sure there's no added sugar!) on two oatcakes and eat them with a glass of water. The butter's fat content should keep you feeling full while the oats give your brain a much-needed glucose top-up to revitalise your body and mind, according to nutritionist Rhiannon Lambert.

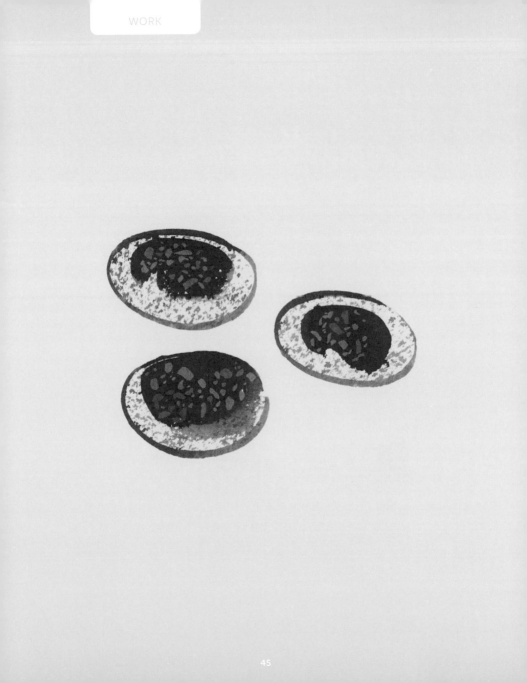

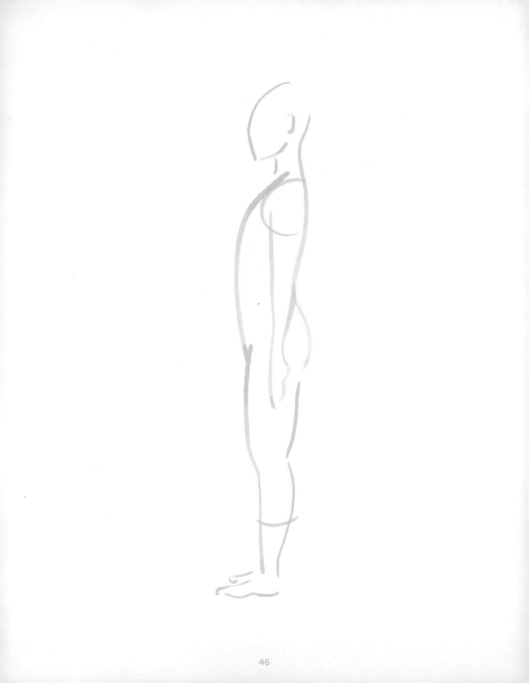

Feign self-confidence

According to Mark Leonard, simply adopting a more upright posture, and focusing on the body rather than the insecurities of the mind, can encourage us to feel more positive and less anxious.

Sit or stand, tilting the pelvis forwards slightly, lifting and opening the chest and tucking in the chin. Breathe in, lifting the shoulders up towards the ears before breathing out, allowing the shoulders to drop and releasing any tension in the upper back and shoulders. Slowly repeat this move three times, taking deep, measured breaths. Then, holding an upright posture, chest open, continue to breathe slowly in and out, noticing the way the chest and shoulders relax as you exhale.

Swerve workplace sniffles

Zinc can
deactivate cold
viruses when taken orally,
preventing them from
attaching to membranes
inside the nose and mouth,
and stopping them from
replicating.

Feel a tickle in your throat or the first signs of a
stuffy nose? Take a zinc lozenge – available at
pharmacies or health-food shops – to decrease
your symptoms and speed up the rate at which
the body naturally combats the cold virus – by
50 per cent according to some experts. Just
make sure you're choosing pure zinc acetate or
zinc gluconate rather than a product with added
vitamin C, citric acid or sorbitol, which make the
lozenge taste nicer but may reduce zinc's benefits.

Be more decisive

This mindfulness exercise by Mark Leonard helps you to clear the mind and become more aware of your true feelings and instincts, enabling you to make better decisions and worry less.

Sit comfortably, with your spine tall but relaxed. Focus on the feelings in the body and, if possible, let go of thoughts about the problem at hand. Notice colours, shapes, sounds and sensations while sitting. Then, when the mind has cleared a little, bring the question or matter to mind and explore the emotions and sensations that come when you consider different options. Can you feel your heart racing? Do you become anxious? Is there past experience you can use to guide you?

Alleviate neck pain

Working at a computer or carrying stress in the shoulders can cause tightness and pain in the neck. This yoga stretch from Amanda Fell lengthens and warms the neck to release tension.

Sit at your desk or kneel on the floor, and rest your hands on your knees with shoulders relaxed. Inhale and bring the chin down to the chest. As you exhale, lean the head to the right, bringing the right ear towards the right shoulder. Inhale to bring the head back up to centre. Repeat on the other side. Do the full movement three times, then exhale and turn your head to the right, inhale back to the front, and then repeat to the left. Repeat the full movement three times.

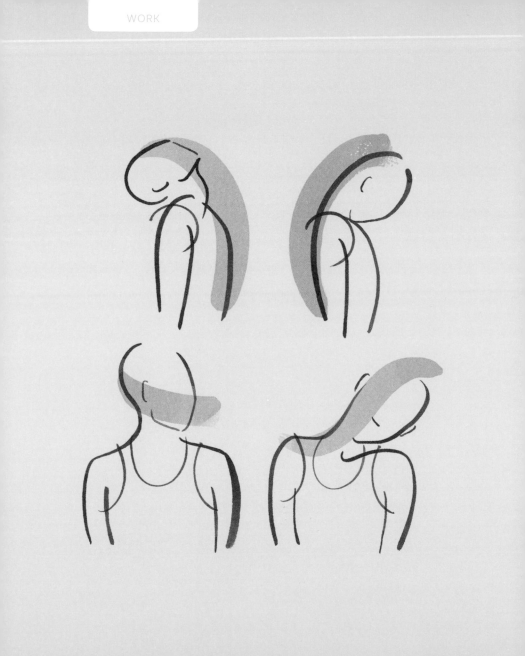

Overhaul office treats

This recipe
by nutrition coach
Monique Cormack
(nourisheveryday.com)
combines coconut and dark
chocolate for a decadently
rich treat to help you
resist sugary snacks.

For a no-cook, no-effort trail mix, combine
½ cup (75g) almonds, a generous sprinkle of
unsweetened coconut flakes and 3 squares of 85
per cent dark chocolate, broken into small pieces.
As well as being tasty, the coconut is rich in fibre
and the cocoa is a good source of antioxidants,
which can have cardiovascular benefits. Stash this
single portion in your desk drawer and reach for
it when the weekly office cupcake run occurs, or
make a larger batch to share with colleagues.

Undo desk damage

Incorporating brief bursts of walking into your daily routine can help offset the health hazards of sitting for hours at a time, which include heart disease, diabetes and early death.

Standing up and engaging in just 2 minutes of casual walking for every hour you spend sitting down has been associated with tangible improvements in overall health – even more so than standing all day. Set an alarm timer on your computer or phone to alert you every hour, and get on your feet when it goes off. The focus isn't speed, it's simply activity, so even walking to the other end of your workplace or going up and down a couple of flights of stairs is enough to reap the rewards.

Focus the mind

This breathing exercise diverts the mind's attention away from worries or distractions and is a good way of practising focusing the brain on one matter at a time.

Sit comfortably and begin to notice your breath. Take the breath deeper, inhaling to maximum capacity and then exhaling slowly. When your mind wanders, just bring it straight back to listening and feeling your breath. Begin to count your inhale, 1, 2, 3, 4, holding the breath for 2 seconds, then exhaling 4, 3, 2, 1. Build the exhale count to 8 to 1, so that your exhale is twice as long as your inhale. Then create a mantra – three powerful, positive words – and repeat these to yourself.

Plant happy thoughts

Green plants within the workplace have been shown to improve satisfaction levels, concentration and even productivity.

Forego a minimalist workplace in favour of bringing a bit of the garden indoors. If space allows it, a small indoor plant on your desk will have the greatest impact, but larger shrubs in communal areas work too. Aloe, spider plants, English ivy and snake plants have all been listed in horticultural studies as species that improve air quality – and they're low maintenance too, which should keep the boss happy.

Say bye to back pain

Stretching out the hamstrings – which become tight from sitting down for prolonged periods – helps to reduce pressure on the spine and alleviate pain in other areas of the body.

On getting home from work, lie on your back and wrap a resistance band or yoga belt around the ball of your right foot. Keeping your left leg stretched out on the floor, pull your right leg up, locking the knee. Hold for 30 seconds and feel the stretch along the back of your leg. Next, take both ends of the band in your left hand, and with the leg still straight and lifted, pull gently to the left. Hold for 30 seconds and breathe through any tightness or discomfort. Repeat both stretches on the left leg.

Pimp up your posture

Swapping your desk chair for a medicine ball can increase calorie burn – and adding quick spine exercises, which increase blood flow to the area, will improve posture and lessen back pain too.

Sit on the ball and raise your arms straight in front of you. Keeping the torso still, move both arms across the body to the right, bending the left elbow and keeping them at shoulder height. Then move both arms to the left, bending the right elbow. Repeat 5 times on each side. Then do the 10-move sequence again, turning the head in the opposite direction to your arms. Finally, spread your feet a little wider and now twist the spine along with your arms, straightening the opposite knee as you move.

Set fluid goals

Staying hydrated will help to improve your mental alertness and mood as well as increasing the efficiency of your immune and digestive systems, says nutrition coach Monique Cormack.

Recommit to the tradition of morning and afternoon tea breaks by setting a reminder on your phone or computer to make a small pot of your favourite herbal tea – to avoid the caffeine jitters – twice a day. Making up a fresh pot in the morning and another in the afternoon will mean you're sipping throughout the working day, which will add around 4 cups (1L) of fluid to your overall intake.

Be more positive

By paying attention to the good things that happen in life, you help the brain create positive neural pathways. This exercise from The Mindfulness Project (londonmindful.com) shows how.

Everyone has an inbuilt negativity bias: our brain concentrates more on the negative stuff that happens to us than the positive. To counter this, we need to focus on positive things – and stay with them for at least 10–20 seconds so that the brain can turn them into neural pathways. So the next time you're feeling grateful for something, really notice it and how it makes you feel. The longer you savour the beautiful moment, the more positive pathways your brain will develop.

Feel more content

This pose allows for a gentle chest opening and calms the nervous system.

Liz Veyhl (smallworldyoga.org) says the Reclining Bound Angle pose is her go-to for relaxation and a sense of well-being. Sit with your back upright and legs stretched straight out in front. Bend your knees and draw your heels in towards your pelvis. Press the soles of your feet together and let your thighs fall open. Lean back, bringing your elbows to the floor, then lower yourself all the way down. Let your arms relax alongside your body, palms up, and breathe naturally.

Stoke creativity

Your creative juices flow most freely when you're doing an activity that lets the mind wander with ease.

Next time you need to whip up your creativity, consider whipping up a batch of cookies. Or puttering in the garden. Or taking a leisurely walk. Activities that are engaging but not too absorbing are ideal as a break when you need to spark out-of-the-box thinking. Doodling might be the best one of all: studies indicate it stimulates areas of the brain that help you analyse information differently. So those stick figures and smiley faces are really an innovative problem-solving technique!

Don't be afraid to try something new

Fear can be a powerful motivation-crusher. This mindfulness task will help you get over the barrier.

When you want to try something new – learning to kitesurf or taking an art class – sometimes fear pops up. But you can knock it back. First, recognise the fear and admit the effects it has (panic, racing heart). Next, ask yourself, what's the worst thing that can happen? You'd look silly? You'd be out some money? It's usually all stuff you'd get past. And if you *did* fail, there's at least one good thing: you'd never have to regret not having tried. Then make a plan to start small and just do it.

Cure a hangover

Coconut water replenishes fluids and electrolytes that the body sorely needs after a hard night's drinking.

Several factors contribute to a hangover: dehydration causes the headache, while alcohol's toxic components irritate the stomach. Which is why a tall glass of coconut water provides relief. It's hydrating and contains heaps of potassium (an electrolyte), as well as neutralising stomach acid. You can buy it at supermarkets, or if you're somewhere tropical crack open a fresh one (though you probably shouldn't be handling a machete in your condition, so ask a friend to do the hacking).

Get better quality ZZZs

The scent of lavender has been shown to decrease blood pressure and heart rate, and increase deep sleep.

For centuries people have filled sachets with lavender and tucked them under their pillows. But the flower does more than just smell nice: research shows lavender's scent can make your body more relaxed, which helps you get to sleep. It also enhances the quality of sleep. Lavender infusions, candles or sachets all do the job, but perhaps the simplest way to reap the benefit is to dab a few drops of lavender essential oil on a tissue and place it under your pillow.

Curb a craving

By taking a few minutes to study your craving when it hits, you'll be better prepared to decide what to do: fulfil it or not.

When the urgent need for a snack strikes, meditation teacher Emma Mills (emmamillslondon.com) suggests asking yourself a few questions. When does the craving happen? How is it experienced (rumbling stomach or unshakeable thoughts of the thing you desire)? What were you doing right before it happened? (Cravings are sometimes a form of avoidance.) Knowing more about why and how you crave means you'll be better able to make a conscious choice: to give in, or not?

Run mindfully

This exercise from The Mindfulness Project helps you connect and be present with your feet and breath while running, which adds a healthy brain boost to your usual jog.

Start your run at a comfortable pace and tune in to the sensations on the soles of your feet: how does the ground feel? Does it change if you switch from running on grass to a hard surface? When your mind wanders, note where it goes (planning, analysing, daydreaming) and then return to the sensations of your feet. Next, note how your breathing becomes faster as you run faster, slower as you lose speed. Don't try to control the breath, just observe with kindness and curiosity.

Detox after a big night out

This twisting pose applies gentle pressure to the internal organs, which improves digestion and helps move out toxins.

·03·

Yoga teacher Liz Veyhl suggests the Twisting Crescent Lunge to help clean up your act after a night out. Get in the position you'd adopt if you were about to start a 100m sprint: right foot between your hands, left leg lunging back. Bring your hands to your chest in a prayer pose, then twist from the navel to the right, chest open, right elbow lifted and looking up. Take five deep breaths. Come back to centre, then repeat on the other side.

Appreciate the little things

You can grow happiness by paying repeated attention to something, and this exercise from The Mindfulness Project focuses that power on the little things in life.

Write down at least 10 little things you love in life (sunny skies, a neighbourhood cat, the scent of spring). To help you remember them, stick the list somewhere you'll see it regularly. Every morning and every evening look at the list and notice and hold on to the good feeling you get as you read it. Keep perceiving new things and adding them. You might want to use a beautiful piece of paper and different-coloured pens, or make a growing 'little things' collage you can admire.

Boost energy for exercise

Peppermint stimulates energy both mentally and physically. Sniff it or ingest it – or do both with a cup of peppermint tea – for a dose of get-up-and-go.

It's way too early. Or it's been a long day. Both are common excuses for not rallying the energy to exercise or slacking once you're out there. A cup of peppermint tea, however, can be a game-changer. Studies have shown that ingested peppermint improves respiratory function, blood pressure and alertness, while smelled peppermint increases stamina and running speed. Plus the cool, menthol smell hits your nose as you're sipping. So put on the kettle and quit making excuses.

Bring joy to your day

This pose – recommended by Paul Cabanis (paulcabanis.com) – is called the Camel. It opens the chest, which helps breathing and boosts mood.

Kneel on the ground with your thighs perpendicular to the floor and put your hands on your hips. Lift the chest and arch your back, looking up and, if possible, backwards. If this is as far as you can go, that's fine – don't overdo it. If you can take the stretch deeper, reach back and place your hands on your feet. It's more important to get length in your back and to open the chest than to lean far back. Maintain the position for at least 30 seconds, breathing in and out normally.

Feel the beat

Music can alter brain activity. Depending on the rhythm, it may make you calmer or more alert.

Studies have shown that tunes with a strong beat fire up the brain and prompt brainwaves to resonate in time with the rhythm. Slow beats cue slow brainwaves, such as those that occur in hypnotic or meditative states. Faster beats rev up faster brainwaves that result in more alert and focused thinking. So the Foo Fighters' 'No Way Back' would be good to rock out to before a test or presentation, while Adele's 'Someone Like You' might be best before bed.

Learn to daydream

Daydreaming often gets dismissed as a waste of time. But if done correctly it sparks creativity and makes you better at planning and goal-driven thought.

Daydreaming helps your brain access information that's normally out of reach. It works best when you envision a goal, as well as the obstacles you must overcome to reach it. So don't just dream, 'I'm going to win the marathon!' and wallow in the glory. Instead, think, 'I'm going to win the marathon, and here's how I'll do it.' Psychologists estimate we daydream for up to half of our waking hours, so spend at least a few minutes of that daydreaming productively.

Get a nature fix

Whether it's a walk in the park or just a leafy view from a window, a dose of greenery reduces stress, increases focus and improves mood.

Studies have shown just *looking* at trees and grass can have a soothing effect. People who can see greenery from their windows recover faster in hospitals and perform better in school. Even viewing a picture of nature lowers blood pressure and sharpens performance. So if you can't get to a park for a jaunt (a proven stress-buster), consider a minute-long gaze out of the window or look at a woodsy photo. It's especially effective in the late afternoon, when attention starts to fall off.

Cure a hangover

Fruit juices restore water and vitamins that alcohol depletes, and the fructose (a natural sugar) in the juice gives the body energy.

Sweet juices – say, apple, cranberry or pomegranate – not only rehydrate, they also speed up the body's metabolism and help it kick out the boozy toxins faster. Stay away from orange, grapefruit and other sour juices though, as their acidic nature can irritate an already inflamed stomach. If juice isn't your thing, you can eat fresh fruit instead. Bananas are high in potassium (an electrolyte that depletes due to alcohol) and they're easy on an upset tummy.

Laugh more

Laughter increases feel-good hormones in the brain, turns off stress hormones, boosts circulation, and helps muscles to relax. That's just the shortlist.

It's no joke: the act of laughing benefits your body big time. It's a terrific stress-buster. Yet the typical adult laughs only 20 times per day. So get yourself a book of knock-knock jokes. Watch a funny DVD. Engage in a tickle battle. Google 'world's best cat videos'. It's lovely to laugh on your own, but the effect is even greater when you giggle with other people (companionship offers its own health perks) so get together some chums or go along to a comedy night to share the joy of laughter.

Watch mindful movies

Seeing a film is a fun way
to unwind. It can also get
you thinking.

You can watch any movie mindfully by being
aware of the emotions it brings out. Consider
what you feel as you watch, and afterwards note
how it affects your state of mind. Mindfulness
expert Emma Mills says her mindful favourites
include *Cloud Atlas* (2012), a film about how the
actions of individuals impact upon one another
in the past, present and future, and *The Truman
Show* (1998), the story of a man who discovers
his entire life is a TV show.

Soaking in a hot bath relaxes the muscles and contributes to faster relief of soreness.

It seemed like a good idea to ride your bicycle 50km (30 miles) on the weekend. Or to take that advanced weightlifting class. But now you're feeling the pain. A hot bath can ease the damage. Make sure the water's not too hot though. Plunge in and – *ahhh* – soak for 20 minutes or so. Feel free to massage particularly sore areas, since the warmth makes the muscles easier to unknot. If you want to add Epsom salts, go ahead. They'll make your bathwater feel silkier.

Recover after a gluttonous meal

You can't undo what has been done, but this mindfulness exercise helps you feel less guilty about it and make better choices in the future.

You did it: you ate the whole thing. However, you don't have to get stuck in regret. Meditation teacher Emma Mills suggests a three-pronged approach to recovery. First is clear seeing: look at what happened and note how you feel (bloated, guilty?). Next is acceptance: it happened and that's OK. Third, be prepared for next time: turn off the TV while eating or put down your knife and fork between mouthfuls, so you're more aware of what you consume.

Show appreciation

Social bonding, like eye contact and attentiveness, promotes the release of the feel-good hormone dopamine, which fosters closeness, happiness and motivation.

Research shows that couples are increasingly naming technology as a negative issue within relationships; time spent on devices is perceived as a barrier to intimacy and appreciation, and leads to feelings of rejection and resentment. To foster intimacy, both partners should agree that for 30 minutes per day, perhaps before bed or first thing in the morning, devices are switched off. Some time out is necessary to ensure relationships remain real rather than virtual.

Tame anger

This RING technique from clinical psychologist Dr Michael Brustein (drbrustein.com) will help to overcome anger by analysing the emotion and placing it in context.

Recognise your anger and how it makes you feel (body tense, blood boiling; wanting to shout, cry or run away). **I**nvestigate the emotion by asking *why* you feel this way: I'm angry because I feel disrespected. **N**ot identifying means then separating yourself from the emotion: I am angry in this moment; the anger, like a cloud, will pass. I have a choice. I can watch it without identifying with it and acting upon it. Ask yourself whether acting on your anger fulfils your ultimate **G**oals.

Re-connect with old friends

Aim to sidestep any resentment or hurt feelings when initially re-establishing contact to put the friend at ease.

Psychologist Anjula Mutanda (anjula.com) says to start from a place of openness and positivity, seeing the reconnection as an opportunity to be embraced, not a chance to unearth the past and any errors made along the way. Reach out to the old friend in the way you feel most comfortable (whether that's online or by phone) by telling them you miss them. Next, issue an explicit invitation to meet in person or chat face-to-face online to demonstrate that you're keen to connect.

Be more open

Communicating your feelings to others requires self-awareness; this exercise from Dr Michael Brustein will help you take the time to observe how you feel and practise telling someone else.

Follow the STOP steps. Be **S**till. Sit in a quiet place and close your eyes. After three deep breaths, **T**ake note of how you feel. Label your thoughts as you would if a friend came to you and said the same things. Unwrap *why* you feel these different emotions. **O**rganise your thoughts by writing them down. If you can, **P**resent your thoughts and feelings to someone, perhaps a good friend, to validate them and help you on your way to feeling understood by others and yourself.

Liven up your libido

Watermelon contains citrulline, which helps increase sex drive and makes intercourse more pleasurable. So give this recipe by nutrition expert Monique Cormack (nourisheveryday. com) a whirl.

Keep your watermelon fix fresh and light – arrange small diced watermelon cubes on a sharing platter, crumble over sheep's-milk feta, sprinkle with torn fresh basil and finish off with a drizzle of extra virgin olive oil and balsamic vinegar. Then tuck in! Or whip up an energising zesty watermelon mocktail with watermelon, a small piece of fresh ginger, a few mint leaves and a handful of ice. Blend, serve and... begin.

Let go of jealousy

This breathing exercise filled with compassion can help you let go feelings of envy without suppressing the bigger issue, says James Milford (themindfulmethod. co.uk).

Relax your body and become aware of your breath. Once settled, rest your attention on the physical sensations in the body caused by jealousy. Are your muscles taut? Is your jaw clenched? Breathe with these sensations, allowing them to play out, noting how they feel. As you feel the difficult emotions and sensations, silently speak words of comfort, such as 'It's OK to feel like this' or 'I know this is painful'. Treat yourself with the same compassion and support you would a loved one.

Make long-distance relationships work

Mutually agree upon and commit to preferred methods of consistent communication, suggests psychologist Anjula Mutanda.

Communication in long-distance relationships should take two forms: scheduled catch-ups and unscheduled but regular clocking-in between times. This two-pronged approach will help you to stay close and prevent anxiety about what's going on in each other's lives from building, nipping incorrect assumptions and toxic feelings in the bud. Together, choose a regular time to Skype you can both look forward to, with shorter updates in between, to build a sense of closeness.

Embrace forgiveness

According to James Milford, offering forgiveness may release us from the resentment of feeling wronged. This mindfulness exercise allows us to show kindness in the face of hurt.

Sit comfortably, focusing on the breath. After a few moments, bring to mind an image of someone whom you're having difficulty forgiving. Inwardly and silently offer them these phrases: 'May you be happy', 'May you be healthy', 'May you be free from suffering', 'May you go through your days with ease'. After saying the phrases five times, shift the awareness to the body and see how it feels to have offered them. Pay close attention to the sensations rather than the thoughts.

Inspire conversation

This therapy technique from Dr Michael Brustein uses the analogy of knocking at someone's door to facilitate friendly exchange with others, encouraging active listening and curiosity.

First, ring the bell; show a willingness to talk. Instead of asking, 'How was your day?' try, 'Tell me three things that surprised you today.' Does the other person seem to want to talk or desire their own space? If they open the door, be curious about their answers and validate their feelings. If they seem to keep the door closed, follow up gently but don't turn away altogether. After they've opened the door to their experience, you can then express you own experience and share the space together.

Feel sexy

Spending time alone, with your body as the focus, helps to normalise its image and shift sexual thoughts from being negative to being positive, says Anjula Mutanda.

In front of a full-length mirror, stand upright and look at your body in its naked state or in underwear. We tend to see the body in sections, and avoid looking at some, but take time to view every part. While you're doing so, notice any negative or judgemental thoughts, then let them go. Focus on thinking about the positive things that your body has achieved, and compliments people have made about it. See if you can think of a new positive every time you do this exercise.

Make the most of mealtimes

This
listening exercise
from integrative
psychotherapist Hilda Burke
helps you to learn to create
space and time to fully enjoy
other people when you sit
down with them
to eat.

When sitting down to dinner with others, leave any digital devices in another room and commit to spending 15 minutes dedicated solely to listening to what they want to say. Upon hearing certain buzz words that resonate, recognise them as a cue to share your own opinions or thoughts on a subject. Starting with 15 minutes, and alternating between being the speaker and the listener, means that there's an awareness of making that time count.

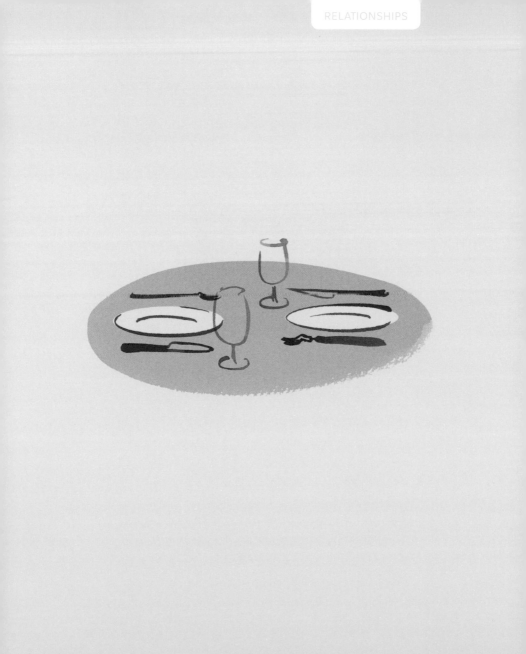

Gain perspective

This mindfulness meditation from expert Mark Leonard helps you to become more familiar with your reaction to challenging situations – and think twice before reacting.

Sit upright, and begin by noting sensations in the soles of the feet. Move on to the feeling of your hands resting in your lap. Now direct awareness to the belly and chest. Next, bring to mind a situation that causes frustration or confusion, and notice what's going on in the body – whether your breathing changes, if any tension builds. Now, if it's possible to do so, just focus on feelings in the body and let thoughts fade into the background before opening your eyes and getting on with the day.

Escape growing resentment

Simple
switches in the focus
and language of the way
you debate with others
can elicit positive change
and prevent cultivating
bitterness, suggests
Hilda Burke.

Whenever you find yourself in a disagreement
or confrontation situation, try to acknowledge
your own part in creating it. By doing this, you're
modelling a mature and productive method of
behaviour for your conversation partner.
In contrast, focusing energy on highlighting their
behaviour, attitude and wrongdoing will encourage
the same from them, and the inevitable result
is a blame game in which both parties feel
unfairly treated.

Keep things fresh

According to Hilda Burke, neither routine nor complacency is a marker of a healthy relationship. Making a conscious effort to maintain a certain level of spontaneity frees us to re-connect with a partner.

Refrain from shutting down your own ideas or a partner's suggestions that don't fit your current routine or reality. Whenever you feel yourself about to think or say, 'We couldn't do...', replace it with, 'Let's do...'. Spontaneity doesn't have to involve doing something that's crazy or elicits high levels of excitement; simply switching up a routine Friday dinner by inviting your partner on a midweek date to a new restaurant can be enough to ward off complacency.

Encourage intimacy

Exploring sensations of touch and feelings in the body inspires a sense of security and connectedness between two people.

Wherever you are with your partner, says expert Mark Leonard, let go of the need to talk. Instead, ground awareness in the body. Allow the mind to wander but keep your awareness on the physical sensations. Make eye contact with your partner and feel the effects of lifting the corners of the mouth into a smile. Enjoy the pleasure sensations as each moment comes and goes, and notice judgements in the mind, but always come back to exploring sensations with no goal in mind.

Foster respect from kids

Using language and behaviours that provide clarity when communicating with children helps to cultivate mutual understanding and respect, says psychologist Anjula Mutanda.

Make the word 'because' your best friend when speaking to youngsters to provide a reason for any instructions you give. This allows children to understand why things are happening, why boundaries are being set, and makes your opinion harder to dismiss. Children become frustrated and irritable when they feel out of control or governed by abstract rules. Using the word 'because' will let them know where they stand and help them to see you as being open and accessible.

Diffuse arguments

This communication technique from Hilda Burke promotes taking turns talking to help create an honest discourse that is less likely to escalate into conflict.

Avoid misinterpreting each other's meaning by taking turns to relay one side of the story while the other person listens silently. The listener should then reflect back to the speaker what they've heard. This is often quite different from what the speaker thought they'd said! Repeat this exercise until each speaker has agreed that the listener has echoed back their words and sentiments correctly. By using this technique regularly, the focused listening skills filter into everyday interactions.

Be present with a partner

According to Anjula Mutanda you can identify verbal cues that point to a person's current emotional state, which can be used to guide conversation and promote closeness and kindness.

Setting mobiles and tasks to one side, begin talking to your partner. When they speak, quieten any responses you form and focus instead on what they say and the words they choose to use. Aim to ask questions that elicit how they're *feeling*, rather than the practicalities of what they've done or plan to do, and pick up on language that suggests emotion. For example, if they say, 'I had a really frustrating conversation', ask, 'Why did you end up feeling that way?' rather than, 'Who else was there?'

Get instant happiness

Smiling is evolutionarily contagious – and the power of this facial action to stimulate the brain's happiness response is catching too!

Whether you're at home or work, out and about in your neighbourhood or on holiday, make an effort to smile at other people, while holding eye contact with them. Smiling has proven biological benefits for the smiler – reduced stress-hormone levels, lower blood pressure, increased mood-enhancing hormone production – and you'll be surprised by how many people react positively. In fact, science confirms that, when smiling, we're perceived to be more likeable, courteous and competent.

Cope with grief

Grieving is a deeply personal experience and follows no set timeline, but writing a journal when it strikes most strongly can help encourage healing.

The grieving process is prolonged when we choose to ignore the pain and seek distractions, says integrative psychotherapist Hilda Burke. Instead, keep a mood diary. Whenever feelings of grief or sad thoughts about what has been lost emerge, note down their existence, with the time and a scale of how painful they seem. This will help you to understand that grief isn't a permanent state, that over time the painful feelings will surface less and less frequently and become less strong.

Plan a trip

Anticipation of a trip boosts happiness more than the trip itself, according to research.

Planning a trip is the best part. The actual excursion may not live up to the fantasy, as jetlag, annoying crowds and family fights can mar it. Furthermore, once home the pleasure evaporates as you fall back into work and daily life. The planning stage, however, allows you to dream. So pick a destination and put it in the calendar. Watch movies about the place. Chat with friends who have been there. It all results in a measurable spike in overall happiness.

Stretch in your airplane seat

Sitting on a flight typically causes you to slouch and keep your spine in one position for too long. This exercise prompts you to lift and rotate the body, bringing circulation and relief.

Yoga teacher Paul Cabanis (paulcabanis.com) suggests a twist in your seat. Sit upright, keeping both feet flat on the ground. Align your head directly over the centre of the pelvic floor. Clasp your left knee with your right hand, and then turn your trunk to the left keeping your feet, legs and hips stable. Gently use your left arm and shoulder to help you turn. Do not turn the pelvis. Ensure that you lift so you don't compress the spine. Maintain for 30 seconds. Repeat on the right side.

Use your commute

This exercise,
from meditation
pro Emma Mills
(emmamillslondon.com),
cultivates present-moment
awareness, which helps the
mind to be calmer, clearer
and more alert.

From the moment you leave your house, be with
your experience as it unfolds. Don't multitask.
If you are walking, be walking, if you are on the
train looking out of the window, do just that; focus
on what's happening now in your sensory world.
It might be helpful to imagine that when you get
to your destination someone is going to ask you to
describe your trip in detail – what you saw, heard,
smelled – so pay attention. This meditation brings
a sense of novelty and joy to a routine event.

Sleep better on an airplane

The closer you get to lying flat, the better it is for your back and neck.

Magical creatures do roam the skies – they're the ones who nod off soon after the wheels go up and slumber peacefully for the flight's duration. For the rest of us, let's talk posture. There's not much wiggle room in an economy seat, but putting your chair back as far as possible creates the optimal position for sleeping (apologies to the person behind you). If you're shorter, you can also rest your legs on your carry-on bag. If you have a couple of little pillows, use them to steady your head.

Stop motion sickness

By targeting acupressure points in the arm, you can balance the body's flow of energy and reduce nausea.

The boat won't. stop. bouncing. A queasy wave-like feeling rises in your stomach. Can you stop it before barfing begins? Yes, and it's pretty simple. Find the point on your inner forearm, three finger-widths down from your wrist crease, between the two tendons. Use your thumb to press here, pushing fairly deep (but not so it is painful). Hold for a few minutes, then do the same to the other wrist. Repeat as needed.

Stay calm while flying

This exercise works by using breathing to focus the mind away from worry. Lowering and resting the head also serves to calm you.

If you're feeling nervous on a flight, Paul Cabanis recommends doing a forward fold. Lower the tray table and rest your forehead on your forearms. Take slow, gentle, slightly deeper-than-normal breaths. The trick is to slow the breathing enough for it to be calming, and to maintain it for as long as needed and you feel comfortable.

Ease sinus pain and headaches in the air

Pressing key points on the face relieves pressure and helps sinuses drain; the latter result also has the perk of keeping germs from taking root.

You've probably heard the usual bag of tricks for staying healthy on a flight: use hand-sanitising gel, stay hydrated, keep your overhead vent on. This acupressure exercise adds to the arsenal by targeting key sinus points. Start by massaging both sides of your nose, by the nostrils, using your index fingers to apply moderate pressure for 2–3 minutes. Now move to the cheekbones, at a point level with the middle of your nose. Again, press with your index fingers for 2–3 minutes.

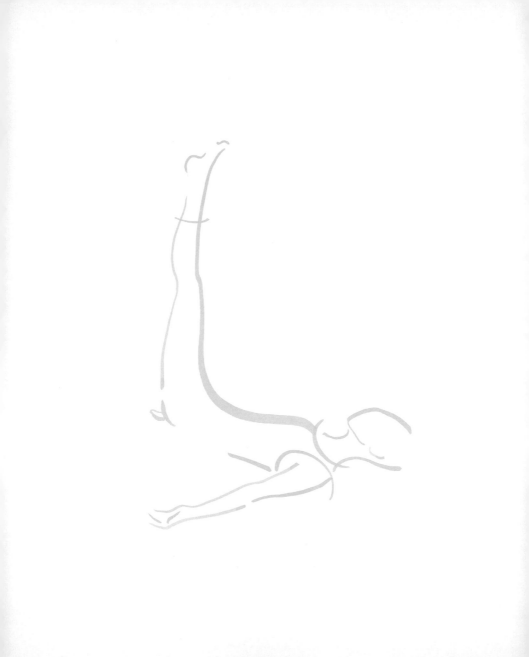

Get rid of jetlag

This exercise helps relieves fatigue, and the inversion counters the pooling of blood and fluids in the feet that can occur during a flight.

Paul Cabanis recommends Legs Up the Wall pose to help beat jetlag. Get a couple of thick folded blankets and place them next to a wall. Sit with your hip next to the wall and your back to the blankets or bolster. Swing gently around so you're lying with the blankets under your back and your bottom is close to the wall. Bring your legs up on to the wall. Open the chest and breathe normally. Stay there, making sure the back remains elevated and chest opened, for 5–10 minutes.

Protein power

Munching
plenty of quality
protein maintains your
energy levels, boosts
concentration and keeps your
immune system functioning
properly at home
and abroad.

Carnivores have lots of protein sources to choose
from, but we're not talking greasy burgers here.
Instead, opt for fish or chicken, since they contain
less saturated fat and cholesterol than red meat.
Eggs are a complete protein, with essential
amino acids, while cheese, yoghurt and other
dairy products also all contain lots of protein.
Vegans can get their fix with a grain-and-legume
combination, such as wholegrain bread spread with
nut butter, or a corn tortilla topped with beans.

Get in vacation mode

Meditation teacher Emma Mills (emmamillslondon.com) reveals here how to practise motivelessness, which can help you switch off from everyday duties and settle in on holiday.

Sit in a chair or somewhere nice and airy. Maybe fetch a cup of tea. Take a few deep breaths, and that's it. Don't force relaxation or getting into vacation mode. Just sit and be with yourself. Maybe you get a desire to go look out the window or make a sandwich. Go ahead. Or not. The idea is to practise being motiveless and operating without an agenda, and to swap an achievement orientation for a pointless-fun orientation. This leaves you open to all kinds of opportunities.

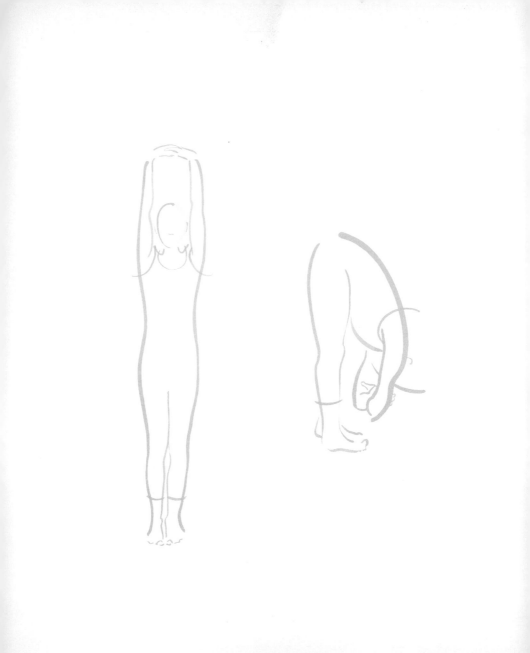

Chill out while waiting in line

These poses are quick-and-easy full-body stretches.

Instead of gnashing your teeth while waiting in line at the airport or a mobbed museum, use the time to stretch and relax. Paul Cabanis suggests 'standing tall': simply bring your legs together and stand upright. Raise up your arms, interlocking the fingers and turning the palms to the ceiling. Alternatively, try a Standing Forward Fold. Spread your feet, bend your knees slightly and fold forwards, clasping your elbows overhead and letting your head hang. Hold for at least 30 seconds.

Soothe sunburn

Plain yoghurt contains probiotics and enzymes that help skin to heal.

Burns happen, despite your best hat-wearing, SPF-slathered intentions. Cold, plain yoghurt not only feels soothing on sunburned skin but also aids its recovery. Get half a cup or so of plain yoghurt (not vanilla) – Greek yoghurt is best, but regular yoghurt will do. Wash your hands, then apply the yoghurt directly to your burn. Leave it on for 5–10 minutes, then rinse it gently away with cool water. Do this three times on the first day that you're sunburned.

Take a pause if feeling overwhelmed

A mindful pause helps you step out of the cycle of worry and distraction so you are better able to relax and think more clearly.

Travel can ramp up stress big time, but taking a mindful pause grounds you. Take a deep breath, letting it move up through your chest. Notice how your body feels, but don't categorise these sensations as good or bad. Next, focus your attention on your breathing, as air touches your nostrils. Just observe it for a few ins and outs. Now re-engage with what's around you. You may still feel anxious, but you've interrupted the feeling and refocused yourself to handle it.

Prevent insect bites

Catnip, a herb in the mint family, has proved in some studies to be more effective than DEET (the compound used in commercial repellents) at repelling pesky mozzies.

No one knows why catnip wards off mosquitoes and other bugs. There's some speculation that they just don't like the smell (which is sort of minty and citronella-like). Health-food stores typically carry catnip essential oil, which is what you want for the job. Most people tolerate it on their skin, but do a patch test first to make sure you aren't allergic. One issue: it wears off after a few hours and needs to be reapplied. And you may have a lot of excited cats following you around…

Comfort irritated skin

The vitamins and healthy fats in olive oil and coconut oil soothe dry patches, while raw potato calms aggravated skin, thanks to its anti-inflammatory nutrients.

Itchy, flaky, red, splotchy – your skin has probably experienced it all while travelling, thanks to factors such as dry air in flight and climates that you're not used to. Olive oil and coconut oil are easy-to-find DIY remedies that you just rub on. Basically, the same antioxidants that make them good to eat make them good for your skin. Raw potatoes are high in vitamin C, potassium, carotenoids and other agents that fight inflammation, so putting a slice on aggravated skin provides quick relief.

Calm insect-bite itches

Basil leaves contain camphor, which has a cool, mentholated effect that stops itchiness.

This one is as simple as it gets: chop up a few fresh basil leaves and rub the bits right on to the bite. It can be helpful for wasp and bee stings, too.

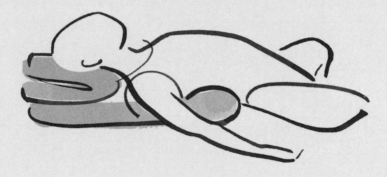

Soothe an upset stomach

This pose elevates the chest above the abdomen and helps the digestive process by creating more space for the organs involved

Paul Cabanis says the following exercise can offer relief for an upset stomach. Place a folded blanket on the ground with additional support under your head. Sit on the blanket, bring the soles of your feet together and lie back on the blanket, arms to the side with palms facing up. While inhaling, focus on the sensations in your chest, and while exhaling, focus on the sensations in your abdomen and pelvis. Continue for 5 minutes.

Ease tired, blistered feet

Green tea is anti-inflammatory, antibacterial and anti-fungal, which means sticking your feet in a tub of tea-infused water reduces puffiness, prevents infections and fights odour.

It's hard work traipsing around Paris or Buenos Aires all day, and your feet are screaming for mercy. Treat them to a green-tea footbath. Brew a strong batch using five or so tea bags, allow it to cool to a pleasing temperature and pour it into a small tub. Now plunge your bare tootsies in and soak away their sorrows for 10–15 minutes.

Relieve neck pain

Rubbing acupressure points in the neck releases localised tension and discomfort.

Ever woken up after snoozing on an airplane or a sandbag hotel pillow with your neck stiff and aching? Here's an easy way to feel better. Stick out your thumbs and put them behind your head on the back of the neck, just below the base of the skull. Your thumbs should be about 7.5–10cm (3–4in) apart. Feel for a small, palpable dent on each side of the neck. *Voilà* – those are the pressure points. Massage them using firm pressure toward the skull for 2–3 minutes, and repeat as needed.

Harness the travel mindset wherever you are

These simple-to-do activities in your 'real' life cultivate the same sense of adventure and bliss you feel while travelling.

One way to globe-trek at home is to try different foods. Try a Burmese restaurant, Jamaican market or Colombian bakery. Likewise, drive to an unfamiliar part of town, walk a few blocks and see what you see. This blends into a third component of keeping the vibe alive: notice the details around you. Novel things surround you at home as well as abroad, but you forget to pay attention. Maybe keep a journal of what you experience. It's all about getting a new viewpoint and being inspired.